Life in ...

A Rock Pool
on the Seashore

Sally Morgan

Chrysalis Children's Books

Contents

Life in ...

A Rock Pool on the Seashore

First published in the UK in 2000 by
Chrysalis Children's Books
An imprint of Chrysalis Books Group Plc
The Chrysalis Building, Bramley Road, London W10 6SP

Paperback edition first published in 2004
Copyright © Chrysalis Books PLC
Text copyright © Sally Morgan 2000
Illustrations by James Field

Editor: Russell McLean
Designer: Louise Morley
Picture researcher: Sally Morgan
Educational consultant: Emma Harvey

ISBN 1 84138 172 1 (hb)
ISBN 1 84138 940 4 (pb)
Printed in Hong Kong
British Library Cataloguing in Publication Data
for this book is available from the British Library.

10 9 8 7 6 5 4 3 2 1 (hb)
10 9 8 7 6 5 4 3 2 1 (pb)

Picture acknowledgements:
Aires/Ecoscene: front cover cl, 14b. Mark Caney/Ecoscene: 17b.
Anthony Cooper/Ecoscene: cover background, 28-29. Simon Grove/
Ecoscene: 15l, 15br. Chinch Gryniewicz/Ecoscene: 11t, 11c, 18t, 29b.
Jean Hall/Sylvia Cordaiy Picture Library: 10-11. Angela Hampton/
Ecoscene: 28c. Ben Hextall/Sylvia Cordaiy Picture Library: front cover cl,
21cl, 23b. John Liddiard/Ecoscene: 3, 23t, 24c, 25, 27b. Papilio: front
cover tl, 6, 7t, 18b, 24t, 26. Ken Preston-Mafham/Premaphotos: 18c.
Rod Preston-Mafham/Premaphotos: 7c, 7b, 13tr, 14t, 17t, 20b, 24b, 27c.
Jonathan Smith/Sylvia Cordaiy Picture Library: 13. Barrie Watts:
front cover br, 12t, 12b, 16t, 16b, 19, 20-21, 22, 22b, 27t.

Words in **bold** are explained in the glossary on page 30.

What is a rock pool?

A rock pool is a pool of water on the seashore. Some seashores are covered in rocks which have fallen from the cliffs above. You can find rock pools on these types of shore.

When the **tide** goes out, seawater becomes trapped between the rocks on the shore, forming a pool. Some rock pools are large and deep, others are small and shallow. The pool is cut off from the sea until the tide rises again.

◀ This yellow sponge is an animal. It lives on the lower parts of the shore, near the sea.

The seashore is a changing place, where the sea meets the land. Seashores are never the same for very long. Sometimes the seashore is covered by salty water and pounded by waves. At other times the shore is exposed to the sun. The plants and animals that live on the seashore are used to living in this changing **environment**.

▲ The sea slater looks a bit like a wood louse. It lives on rocks high up on the shore.

◀ These odd-looking animals are called lightbulb sea squirts.

Inside a rock pool

A rock pool is a miniature sea world. Animals and plants live in the rock pool together, waiting for the tide to return.

The rocks around the pool are covered with mussels, limpets and barnacles. Inside the pool there are lots of hiding places for other animals. Large animals, such as crabs and octopuses, crawl under the rocks on the bottom of the pool. Tiny periwinkles creep into the **crevices** between the rocks.

brown seaweed

red seaweed

mussels

starfish

blenny

topshell

prawn

crab

sponge

Seaweeds cover some of the rocks. Their fronds dangle in the water of the pool. Hiding between the fronds are larger periwinkles, topshells and whelks. Fish, prawns and shrimps hide in the shadows of the rocks.

oystercatcher

periwinkle

green seaweed

pipefish

barnacles

brown seaweed

hermit crab

sea anemones

butterfish

crab

limpet

sea urchin

Turning tides

The sea level is always changing. Twice a day, the tide rises up the shore and then goes back again.

Rock pools on the lower shore are cut off for just a few hours when the tide goes out. But rock pools high up on the shore may be cut off for several days.

▶ At low tide, the whole of the shore is uncovered. The animals and plants are exposed to sun, rain, drying winds and even snow.

▶ At high tide, the sea moves up the shore. It covers everything with salty water. When the tide starts to go back out, the upper shore is left exposed until the next high tide, 12 hours later.

Twice a month, a very high tide comes further up the shore. This is followed by a very low tide. These tides are called the **spring tides**. One week later come the **neap tides**. These are smaller tides, when the sea does not move far up or down the shore. Seashores along the Pacific and Atlantic Oceans have very high and very low tides. On the shores of the Mediterranean Sea, the difference between high and low tide is less than one metre.

A tough life

The plants and animals in a rock pool have a tough life. For several hours, while the tide is out, they are exposed to the heat of the sun.

The heat makes the water in the rock pool start to **evaporate**. The pool becomes warmer and more salty. There is less **oxygen** for the animals to breathe.

▲ Out of the water, a beadlet anemone looks like a red blob.

Each animal has its own way of surviving out of the water. The beadlet anemone pulls in its tentacles to protect them. It pushes them out again when it is covered by water. The limpet is a type of snail. It clamps itself firmly to a rock, and is almost impossible to move. This stops it from drying out.

◄ Underwater, a beadlet anemone extends its **tentacles** so it can feed.

▲ Limpets and whelks have heavy shells to protect their bodies from crashing waves.

▼ When the tide returns, waves crash into the pool. Animals have to hang on tight to avoid being swept away.

Seaweeds

The rocks around the rock pool are covered by seaweed. Seaweeds are plants, but they do not have roots like garden plants. Instead, they have a **holdfast** which grips the rock. Their leaves are called **fronds**.

▲ Seaweeds are attached to the rocks by their holdfast.

The seaweeds on the seashore are like trees in a forest or grasses in a meadow – they are a source of food for many of the animals that live on the shore. Like all plants, seaweeds make their own food using sunlight. This is called **photosynthesis**.

◀ When seaweeds are covered by water, the fronds float. This allows them to catch the sunlight.

Seaweed fronds are rubbery and covered in slime. This makes them very slippery! They have to be tough to withstand the crashing waves. The slime stops water evaporating from the fronds. This allows them to survive out of water for a long time. Some seaweeds dry out completely at low tide. When the tide returns, they swell up again.

There are three types of seaweed on the shore. Green seaweeds live in shallow water. Brown and red seaweeds are found in deeper water.

◀ At low tide, the seaweeds are left lying in heaps on the rocks.

▲ Brown seaweeds are found on the lower and middle shore.

Web of life

Snails eat seaweed and crabs eat snails. This is a **food chain**. A food chain shows who eats whom. The seaweeds are always at the bottom of the chain.

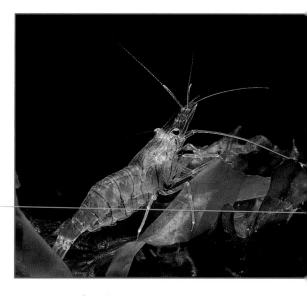

▲ This prawn is feeding on sea lettuce.

Microscopic plants and animals float in the water of the rock pool. They are called **plankton**. Plankton are at the bottom of the food chain too, because they are eaten by larger animals such as barnacles.

Plant-eating animals are called **herbivores**. They eat the plants in the pool. Most of the snails are herbivores. For example, limpets graze on **algae** that cover the rocks. Periwinkles eat seaweed.

◀ This sea anemone has trapped a small prawn in its sticky tentacles.

The herbivores are eaten by meat-eating animals, such as crabs and starfish. Meat-eaters are called **carnivores**. When animals die, their bodies are eaten by **scavengers**, such as prawns and sea cucumbers.

There are many food chains in the rock pool. The food chains link together to form a **food web**.

Here are two typical food chains:

- Seaweed is eaten by periwinkles, which are eaten by starfish.

- Plankton is eaten by barnacles, which are eaten by dog whelks.

▲ Limpets and periwinkles feed on a thin film of algae that covers the rocks.

▼ This fireworm (on the left) is eating the soft body of a cockle.

Plant-eaters

There are many types of herbivores living in the rock pool. Some feed on seaweed while others eat the plankton that floats in the water.

Limpets, periwinkles and whelks are all types of snail. A snail eats with its tongue, which is called a **radula**. The radula is covered with tiny teeth. This makes it rough like sandpaper. A snail uses its radula to scrape algae from the rocks and to break up seaweeds.

▲ The limpet leaves behind a clear trail when it moves.

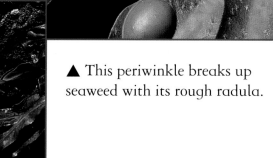

▲ This periwinkle breaks up seaweed with its rough radula.

◀ Limpets use their radula to eat algae.

18

Barnacles, clams, mussels and fan worms are all **filter feeders**. They suck water into their bodies and filter out any plankton. Then they expel the waste water. Barnacles are related to crabs. They live inside a shell which is fixed to the rocks. When they are covered by water, they push out their feathery arms to trap plankton.

▲ Barnacles use their feathery arms to sieve plankton from the water.

Crustaceans

A **crustacean** is an animal which has a heavy shell. The shell protects its soft body. There are several different types of crustacean in the pool.

The smallest crustaceans in the pool are fairy shrimps. They have see-through bodies. Some of the largest are crabs and lobsters. A crustacean's shell cannot grow. When the animal grows larger, it casts off its old shell. This is called **moulting**.

▲ This crab has cast off its old shell. The new shell is soft and takes several days to harden.

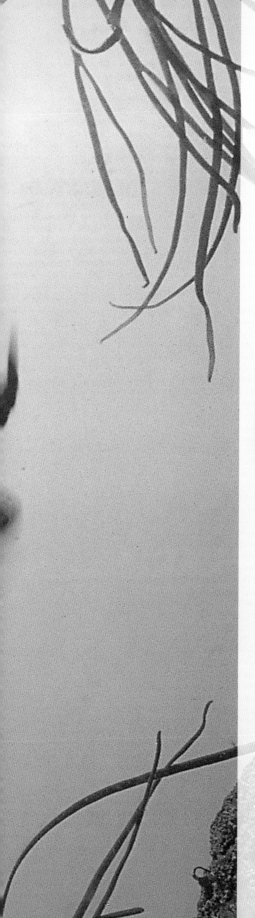

The hermit crab does not have a hard shell. It protects its soft body by living in the shell of a dead whelk. When the crab grows larger, it has to find a bigger shell to move into.

▲ This hermit crab is using the shell of a whelk as its home.

Crabs are hunters. Their flat bodies allow them to hide easily. They squeeze under rocks or burrow into the sand. They have powerful claws to grab their **prey** and pull it to pieces. They have eight legs which bend underneath them. This means they have to walk sideways.

Arms, feet and tentacles

Some very odd-looking animals live in rock pools. Some look like flowers with waving tentacles. Others are spiny balls that hide in holes in the rocks.

The sea urchin is round and covered in long spines. It uses the spines to wear away a small hollow in the rock where it can hide. It has long feet like tubes. They stretch beyond the spines and help the sea urchin to move around. It has jaws for eating small plants.

▼ A sea urchin is completely covered in long, needle-like spines.

A starfish has a spiny coat for protection. It does not have a head, but there is a mouth on its underside. The starfish moves using its tube-like feet. Each foot is filled with water. If one arm is damaged or pulled off, the starfish grows a new one. This is called **regeneration**.

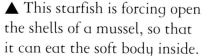 This starfish is forcing open the shells of a mussel, so that it can eat the soft body inside.

▼ The sting from the tentacles of this sea anemone can kill small animals in the rock pool.

The sea anemone has a bag-shaped body with a mouth in the middle. Around the mouth are lots of tentacles. Each tentacle is covered in stinging cells. The anemone uses its sting to **paralyse** its prey, such as small fish and prawns. Sea anemones are related to jellyfish. Jellyfish live in deeper water, but occasionally one may get trapped in the rock pool.

Molluscs

Snails, limpets, clams, sea slugs and octopuses all belong to a group of animals called **molluscs**.

▲ The mussel has two shells. It sucks in water through a tube.

All molluscs have soft bodies. Many of them have a hard outer shell. The smallest molluscs are dog whelks, periwinkles and topshells. They are all snails with a single shell. Some have a simple cone-shaped shell, but most have a spiral shell. Sea slugs are snails without a shell.

▼ The bright colours of a sea slug show it is **poisonous** to eat.

▼ The topshell has a cone-shaped shell.

Some molluscs, such as mussels and clams, have two shells. They are called **bivalves**. They survive when the tide goes out by pulling their two shells tightly together.

Sometimes an octopus gets trapped in the pool. This mollusc has eight **tentacles**. Each one is covered in suckers. The octopus is a **predator** which feeds on crabs, lobsters and fish. It holds the prey in its tentacles, and then injects a poison with its bite.

Fish life

Small fish live in the rock pool. The pool is a dangerous place for them. Waves may smash the fish against the rocks. Sometimes they are caught by seagulls.

Fish can breathe underwater because they have **gills** on the sides of their heads. They swallow water and then force it through their gills. The gills absorb the oxygen in the water. Nearly all animals need oxygen to survive.

Fish have a streamlined shape to help them swim quickly. Fins help the fish to steer and to stay the right way up in the water.

▼ The blenny is a predator. If there is no prey in one rock pool, it crawls to another.

The scorpion fish has spines on its back and over its gills. They protect the fish from attackers.

▼ The suckerfish grips the rocks with a sucker on its underside.

Each fish **adapts** to life in the rock pool differently. The blenny uses stiff fins to crawl across the rocks, from pool to pool. The suckerfish has a pair of fins which act like a sucker. They help it to hang on to rocks, and stop it from being swept away by the tide. The pipefish is a long, thin fish. It lies hidden among seaweed. If it stays still, it is almost impossible to spot.

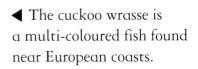

◄ The cuckoo wrasse is a multi-coloured fish found near European coasts.

Save our shores

Seashores are under threat. More people visit them every year. Holiday-makers climb over the rocks, harming the animals and trampling the seaweeds.

Sometimes, people collect animals and take them home in buckets. Litter is left on the shore by visitors, and is washed up with the tides. Many birds become entangled in old nets and pieces of plastic.

▲ The tide brings all sorts of rubbish on to the shore. Some of it, especially old fishing nets, can harm wildlife.

In many parts of the world, raw **sewage** is piped out to sea. The sewage contains harmful **bacteria**. It poisons crabs, lobsters, prawns and mussels. This means we cannot eat them.

◀ This seashore has been turned into a marine nature reserve. This protects the wildlife and stops people from dumping waste.

Oil **tankers** carry huge quantities of oil around the world. In an accident, oil may be spilt into the sea. The oil floats on the surface of the water and washes up on the shore. The black, sticky liquid covers the rocks and kills animals and plants. It may take up to ten years for the shore to recover.

◀ These people are trying to clear a thick layer of oil that is covering a beach.

Glossary

adapt To become suited to an environment.

algae Simple plants which float in water. They range from microscopic plants to large seaweeds.

bacteria Tiny, single-celled organisms that are too small to be seen with the naked eye.

bivalve A mollusc that has two shells, such as a clam or a mussel.

carnivore An animal that eats other animals.

crevice A narrow opening.

crustacean An animal with a heavy protective shell and ten legs.

environment The surroundings of an animal or a plant.

evaporate To change from a liquid to a gas – as when liquid water turns into water vapour.

filter feeder An animal that feeds by filtering plankton from water, using its tentacles, gills or feathery arms.

food chain A series of living things which depend on each other for food. A typical food chain begins with a plant which is eaten by a plant-eating animal. The plant-eating animal is then eaten by a meat-eating animal.

food web All the different food chains in an environment.

frond The leaf of a seaweed.

gills The openings on the sides of a fish's head. A fish breathes by taking in water through its gills.

herbivore An animal that eats only plants.

holdfast A type of root which anchors seaweed to rocks or the sea bed.

microscopic Too small to be seen with the naked eye.

mollusc An animal that has a soft body, a shell and a large muscular foot for moving.

moulting Shedding a shell or skin.

neap tide A small tide which happens twice a month.

oxygen A colourless gas in the air. Most animals and plants need oxygen to live.

paralyse To prevent an animal, or part of an animal, from moving.

photosynthesis The way green plants make their own food using sunlight. The leaves use light energy to combine carbon dioxide and water to make sugar and oxygen. Plants use the sugar as fuel.

plankton Microscopic plants and animals that float in water.

poisonous Harmful.

predator An animal that hunts other animals for food.

prey An animal that is hunted by other animals for food.

radula A mollusc's rough tongue.

regeneration The regrowth of part of an animal or plant.

scavenger An animal which feeds on the remains of food left by other animals. Scavengers also feed on dead bodies.

seaweed Simple plants that grow in saltwater. They have a holdfast instead of roots. Their leaves are called fronds.

sewage Waste from bathrooms and kitchens which empties into drains.

spring tide Very high tides which happen twice a month.

tanker A large ship which carries oil.

tentacles The arms of a sea animal such as an octopus. Tentacles may be used to feel, hold, move or sting.

tide The rise and fall of the sea, which happens twice a day.

FURTHER READING
Some titles may be out of print and available only in libraries.

Collins Complete British Wildlife Photoguide, Paul Sterry, Harper Collins, 1997.
Collins Pocket Guide: Sea Shore of Britain and Northern Europe, Peter Hayward, Tony Nelson-Smith & Chris Shields, Harper Collins, 1996.
Eyewitness Guides: Shell, Alex Arthur, Dorling Kindersley, 1989.
Junior Nature Guides: Saltwater Life of Great Britain and Europe, Leslie Jackman, Dragon's World, 1995.
Junior Nature Guides: Seashells of Great Britain and Europe, R. Tucker Abbott, Dragon's World, 1993.

Index